**For the glorious Whippys
S.G.**

**For Louisa and Daniel
A.C.**

First published in 1996

First published in Great Britain in 1996
by Macdonald Young Books
61 Western Road
Hove
East Sussex
BN3 1JD

Typeset in Bembo 20pt by Goodfellow and Egan Ltd, Cambridge
Printed and bound in Belgium by Proost International Book Production

British Library Cataloguing in Publication Data available.

ISBN: 0 7500 1907 7
ISBN: 0 7500 1908 5 (pb)

SALLY GRINDLEY

SHIPSHAPE

Illustrated by Allan Curless

MACDONALD YOUNG BOOKS

Shipshape was a ship's cat. She spent her days on board
a tug boat, *The Jolly Seasaw*. She was Jim's "special".
Ten years old but young at play. Jim was the skipper,
Shipshape was his mate.

On hot, calm days, Shipshape perched at the bow of
The Jolly Seasaw, eyes closed, nose in the air, taking in
the sun, looking like a figurehead. The salt from the sea
spray coated her fur and whiskers and she liked the taste
when she licked them clean. When other boats bobbed
by, their people waved to her, for Shipshape was
well-known among the harbour folk.

On cold winter days, she snuggled down by Jim at the helm. She could hear the wind howling but she was warm and cosy. She could hear the waves crashing against the side of the tug, but she was safe and Jim talked to her about this and that and the other.

Sometimes Jim let her hold the wheel. On hind legs,
back arched, head high, her front paws felt each turn –
to port, to starboard, left, right – with Jim standing
close behind, just helping a little.

When fisherfolk passed, they threw fish for Shipshape's supper. Jim cooked it with milk, not too fast and not too long. Shipshape smelled the fishy smells and rubbed round Jim's legs until the feast was put before her and she savoured every mouthful.

At times like this Shipshape purred her contentment.
She couldn't meow. She had never meowed. Jim kept
saying the cat had got her tongue, but she didn't
understand what he meant or why he always laughed.

One day, Jim and *The Jolly Seasaw* had difficult work to do. A giant oil tanker had broken down. *The Jolly Seasaw* had to tow it into harbour to be repaired. It was a dangerous job because there were rocks all around.

It was a warm day but the sea was rough. Shipshape prowled the decks of the tug. There was nothing she could do to help but she liked to look important.

She watched as Jim and the skipper from another tug
threw ropes to the men aboard the tanker. She watched
as they tied them fast. She watched as Jim went back to
the cabin to start the engine up. She watched as the rope
suddenly pulled tight and tripped up Tigger Tom, one
of Jim's men. She watched as he plunged into the
swirling sea.

No one else was watching. No one else heard him shouting for help. *The Jolly Seasaw* began to move away. The tanker began to move after the tug. Shipshape smelled danger in the air. The twitch of her whiskers told her something was wrong.

"MEOW!" Shipshape meowed.
Shipshape ran to Skipper Jim and meowed
and meowed.

"Not now, Shipshape," said Jim.
"I've got difficult work to do." Then he gasped and said, "Shipshape, you meowed!"
Shipshape meowed again, then ran away. She stopped and waited for Jim to follow. Jim looked puzzled.

Shipshape went back up to him, then ran away again and waited.

"Well, bless my soul!" said Jim. "She's trying to tell me something!"

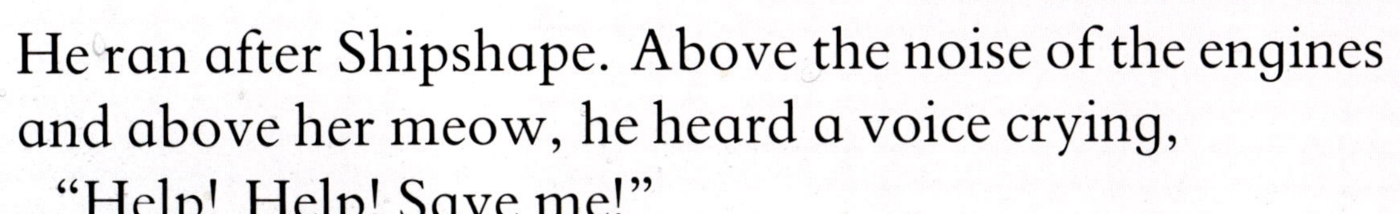

He ran after Shipshape. Above the noise of the engines
and above her meow, he heard a voice crying,
 "Help! Help! Save me!"
 Skipper Jim looked, and saw Tigger Tom gasping
 for breath as he struggled to keep his head
 above the waves.
  "Hold on, Tom," he yelled. "We'll save you!"

Shipshape watched as Jim rushed to turn off the engine.
She watched as he screamed at the other tug to stop.
She watched as he hurled a lifebelt down to
Tigger Tom and hauled him to safety.

Everyone else was watching too and how
they cheered and cheered. Jim called
Shipshape to him. He lifted her gently in
the air and said, "Here's the real hero.
Shipshape saved Tigger Tom. She's
found her tongue at last."

That night, Tigger Tom brought her an enormous cod
and Jim cooked her the biggest bowl of milky fish she
had ever had. Shipshape smelled the fishy smells and

rubbed round Jim's legs. When the feast was set
before her, she savoured every mouthful and
purred her contentment.

Now when other boats bob by, their people salute her, for Shipshape is famous among the harbour folk. And when Jim hears her meow, he always pays attention because he knows she won't make a fuss unless she has something important to say.